Preface:

This book will teach you to reach the state of financial independence in the '20s. This book is written through my experience in my life. How I get financially independent at the age of 21. In my perspective, Financial independence is a state of honor for adults. I started at the age of 17. I struggled a lot to achieve this place. I achieve the state after 4 years because I don't know what to do, where to do, how to do, and when to do. Firstly I started with drop shipping. I don't get orders for months. Even I didn't lose hope but lost my money. After 8 months, I decided on a decision. I try this one for last. If it fails, I will drop it. I have gone through many expert blogs and YouTube videos and concluded. I update my site with these ideas. After 15 days of update, my phone rings and notify that an order was placed in my store. After that, I started to print on demand, merch by amazon, and Amazon FBA. Currently, I am studying the stock

First Step towards the sky

Before starting to the steps, Many of you have already known that there are two types of income. One is an active income and another one is passive income. Active income means you are doing something to receive that income. Once the income has been received, the work can't make any more income. While in the case of passive income, you have to work only once. Then the work will generate the income with little to no effort. Why I mention the little to no effort means even in the passive income you have to work to make your income more sustainable.

In this book, I am have only attached the passive income techniques to reach the financially independent. For your kind information, I would like to inform you that to generate passive income is not so easy and not so difficult. I need more work, more concentration, and more confidence. But no need to worry about the above kinds of stuff. Because you will not face the major problems that I have faced. You may need to face new problems. you can easily solve that by yourselves if you follow the book tips and tricks in your model. Even after 2 years, You can also advise others. I strongly believe that Development means not only my development but also the development of people around me. If you people around you developed, Your society will get developed. If your society gets developed, the country will develop.

The first step is an investment. Investments not like stock market investment or crowdfunding investment. Investment means invest in yourself to get skillset. Suppose you are good at writing or if you are interested in writing invest in some writing courses to get evolute the skillset.

There are three kinds of people in the world. Highly motivated people, Highly practicable people, people those who do not come in the above two categories. Some of the people have natural talents who did not come into the category. Highly motivated people – they will do anything if they decide even though they don't know about it. Highly motivated people – they will also do anything only after the rigorous practice.

Example: Highly Motivated type man is not a marathoner but he wants to finish it. He will finish the marathon with some scratches and sprain. Moving to the second type, If they decided, they will practice it for considerable periods. They will participate in the marathon, They will also succeed without any scratches and sprain. Because they have already doing it for months. So they are not affected by these factors.

You have to invest in yourselves to equip the skillset which is needed by the market. This is the first step where I get lagged. I decided and start the business, I didn't equip any skills or ideas to survive. By God's Grace, I didn't lose confidence. Why am I told to start in your teens means you have a family to support your needs such as food, shelter, and clothing.

"Patience is a key element of success"

-Bill gates.

Nowadays there are a lot of opportunities to equip new skills such as Udemy. Have you all know the story of the Khatabook app. Nowadays the app record 20,000 transactions a month. The developer, Vaibhav Kalpe was not related to the IT stream. But he equipped the skill with Udemy. He wants to develop an app to help his dad to maintain his shop account. He learns the android app development from Udemy. He developed and upload it to the play store. An investment company approach him and invest in his company. Now he owns in millions.

By this story, you will come to know that how the skill set equipment is important. Equip a skill that you have an interest in. Suppose you have an interest in developing, equip the developing skill. Suppose You have an interest in music, Equip the musical skills. Suppose You have an interest in writing, Equip the writing skill.

Here I mention five High demand skills that will make money forever and where to start it for free.

1. Social media marketing

2. Copywriting

3. Search Engine Optimization

4. Web development or android development

5. Graphic designing

Social media marketing:

Socialmedia marketing is a type of marketing that uses social media as marketing.In social media marketing, you will learn about the difference between socialmedia. Where we want to do marketing for which products. There is much social media marketing course on YouTube for free. You can learn by paid courses at Udemy at a cheap rate. If you want your results to quickly join in the turn email marketing, it is the best way to learn email marketing. Once you paid, you will get access to their tools and they gave you mentor support and everything you want as a beginner.

Copywriting:

Copywriting is the act or occupation of writing the text for advertising or other forms of marketing. Even some of the big companies pay $300 for a single page of copywriting content. It is an important skill for everyone to advertise their products. You can learn this skill for free kopywritingkourse.com but you

can learn only the basics of the skill. Invest more in yourselves and earn more. This is skill needs rigorous practice too.

Search Engine Optimization:

Search engine optimization is the process of improving the quality and quantity of website traffic to a website or a web page from search engines like google, yahoo, ping, etc. Google page rank algorithm plays a major role in this skill. You need to optimize the metadata of the website to rank the website on the first page of google search. Recently Google has released his free guide for SEO.

Web Development:

Web development is the work involved in developing a Web site for the Internet or an intranet. Web development can range from developing a simple single static page of plain text to complex Web-based Internet applications. Web development includes WordPress web development also. Today most of the websites are developed using WordPress only. WordPress has many tools that are easy to use too. You can learn web development for free on the website freecodecamp.org. You can even sell the template in websites.

Graphic designing

Graphic design is the process of visual comm Graphic design is the process of visual communication and problem-solving through the use of typography, photography, iconography, and illustration. Graphic design help us in many ways such as designing print on demand T-shirt, creating vector images and creating a banner, etc.

If you don't any ideas to learn any skill, you should learn one of the above skills. These are high demand skill is now a day. Suppose you don't have faith in me, just google high demand skill in 2020. You will find the results and compare the results with my suggestions. Always remember "The more you invest in yourselves, the more you gain in the future". Make sure that the course or training is worth the investment. Analysis yourselves more and more and equip the skill of your interest.

If you make interest as your profession, you will never fail in that and also you will never get bore in that. Suppose you don't have any specific interest, equip the anyone of the above skill.

Setup The Basic Needs for business

"**The wealthy buy luxuries last, while the poor and middle-class tend to buy luxuries first. Why? Emotional discipline**"

- Robert Kiyosaki

while equipping the skillset of your interest, you have to set up the basic needs for earning. You have to use your pocket money inefficient ways such as prefer the computer to the bike. The bike is a liability for our age. We don't have any major usage on the bike except roaming. Likewise, you have to improve your financial discipline. Of course, we want a bike but we have to buy it on our own money. Buy a medium-range phone and use the remaining amount in buying online tools. We can buy a premium phone with our own money when we started our earning journey. Mobile is not so important in the journey. It also plays a role in the journey. So, my suggestion is to buy a medium-range phone. Suppose your journey depends on mobile means, Buy a premium mobile. Spend the money according to your journey. Prefer a camera to a gaming console.

Secondly, you need an Id proof that was issued by the government to register and receive payments. All of the business needs the ID proof for the registration process. To start an earning journey, you need ID proof otherwise you will be in vain.I was also lagged in this place. I don't have an Id proof for the registration process in many platforms and then I applied for the ID proof. I had lost many opportunities because of a lack of ID proof. Because of this reason, I started my journey six months later even after I found my interest.

After getting the ID proof, create a bank account in your name. Because you will get payments from your clients or website in online payment only. If you don't have an account how will get paid? Suppose you have an account in the name of your father, it will not look professional. At least open a joint account. I lost nearly $ 20 for this cause. I have an account at UC we media. I wrote posts in the UC we media and generate up to $20. But I don't have a bank account and pan card to withdraw it. When I got that both, the website gets closed. Nowadays it is easy to open a bank account, you can even open an account in online itself. Some banks have digital bank account services with net banking and mobile banking facilities too. So it is important to have a bank account.

Setting your Income to generate

After completing steps one and two, here comes your final step "Setting your income ". In this segment, I am going to share the tips and tricks that I have used to set the business model. The following methods used by me to create a passive income.

1. Drop shipping

2. YouTube channel

3. Print on demand

4. Amazon KDP

5. Selling an online course

I listed them according to investments. We are going to learn about the step by step process included in each process that I have followed to succeed in the field. Some of you have interested in photography and graphic design, you also have an income method which I have attached at last. Because Now Only I start working in those fields.

Drop shipping:

"Don't find customer for your products, find products for your customers."

— Hyacil Han

Dropshipping is a process of product fulfillment that occurs directly from the manufacturer or wholesaler to the customer when the order is placed on a third-party retailer's website or over the phone, circumventing the traditional retail supply chain.

I started my business model with Walmart and eBay. Because you don't need to pay for a subscription to sell products. My first order was placed after 6 months but you don't need to worry about that Because you will know my tips and tricks that are gained by me only after 6 months.

Tip 1: Product Research

Research for product to sale. Product research can be easily done by many online tools that are mostly paid such as algopix. I started my research with google trends.Google trends provide you the data that trends day wise, week wise and month wise.

1. Select a product on ebay which sells more than 25 times.

2. Now search the topic in the google trends whether it trends or not.

3. This process needs more and more patience to select the products.

4. If the product is trending, Note it down and again search for other products.

5. Likewise, do the research for at least for 10 products.

Now search the product in Walmart, Alibaba, Aliexpress. I used Walmart and sometimes I use some third-party websites such as dharavimarket.com, dharavibiz.com. do search for product in google and find the optimized prize for the products.

Listing & Pricing:

After selecting the products. Now open an e-bay website in a new tab. Search the title of your products in e-bay. There will be product listing related to your products. You can also see the products you selected for dropshipping. E-bay is the primary home of most of the drop shippers. Open the products that have at least 10 sales. Keep it aside.

Now you have to sign up to your e-bay seller account. There will be a search box in the page. Type your products and click the search button. There will be a button named as "continue without selecting a product". A window will open to add the products. Copy and paste the details of the product that you selected in above step.

Prizing is an important process in the drop shipping. You have to compete with competitor's prizes. To select the prizes of your product, you need to go through the product that you select for listings. You need to go through the prizes and set an optimized prize.

For example:

If the low price of your competitors is $ 60, you need to set the prizes at $59.55. if you reduce your prize cheaper, the customers will think your product as a low-quality product.

Currently, I am doing dropshipping using Shopify. because the profits are more than e-bay but it needs some investments. After generating revenue from e-bay and shifts to Shopify. Use paid tools for product research and pricing of products. There are many tools available online and even you can automate the process.

First, do the free process and gains some revenue to motivate yourselves and some confidence. If you can invest, you can invest and do this business even in amazon too.

Invest more to reduce the requirements of the work in the dropshipping process. Once you automate the process, you just want to pay for the tools only.

YouTube Channel:

The nice thing about this idea is that even if you make next to nothing, you'll probably have fun doing it. Meanwhile, your friends and family will probably enjoy watching them.

This isn't a get-rich-quick idea, but more along the lines of a get-rich-slowly idea. But better slow than never, and so now might be as good a time as any to buy a hammock and start thinking of passive income ideas and ways to get rich while (mostly) not working.

This can't generate the income instantly. You have to work hard to get more subscribers. Once you reached certain subscribers,

YouTube will automatically promote your videos.

Do videos regularly for 35 days. YouTube will automatically promote your videos. You will also get 1000 subscribers automatically.

The following two steps are the most important step in creating a youtube channel, your channel should have logo and cover image. So that you channel will look professional.

Suppose you have no idea of making videos. You can probably do music videos. First, you want background music and photos.

Music:

You have to use royalty-free music so that you can avoid copyright issues. To get a piece of royalty-free music, you need to go to the YouTube music library where you can find royalty-free music. You need to search for music of your choice. I recommend to make music of topics such as inspirational, motivational, calm music, sleeping music, etc. you have to go through at least 50 to 60 pages and select 4 to 5 music of your choice. From this music itself, you can extend for 1 to 3 hours. If you have enough money to invest, you can buy royalty-free music in Itunes.

Images:

you need to have free high-resolution images. You can download it for free from websites like unsplash.com, freepik.com,vecteezy.com, etc. you have to give attribution to the images. Some of you may not know about the attribution. Attribution is some type of recognition for the creator. If you have money to invest you no need to give attribution. You can buy a stock photo from Shutterstock, Alamy.com, etc. you need to pick 5 to 8 photos fro videos. You can also put a high definition video instead of photos. You can download it from pexels.com, pixababy.com, etc.

Softwares:

You need to have video editing software to edit the video. If you already have any software just skip this step. Otherwise, You can use two free video editing software. One tool is an offline tool and another tool is an online tool. The offline tool is openshot, online tool is clideo. You can use the tool which is more convenient to you. If you don't know about editing, don't worry about it. Youtube has many videos about video editing. I am also learning from that only.

Now you have to upload the video to your channel. to monetize your videos, you need to have 1000 subscribers and 4000 watch hours. After achieving this, you need to have a Google Adsense account. After opening the account, you will have the monetize option in the videos. Approximately you need to wait for at least 2 to 3 months to achieve the monetization. You have to remember one thing that income from Youtube is not a standard one, it depends on many factors.

To increase subscribers :

1) To get more subscribers, you need to reach more viewers. To reach more viewers, you need to optimize the metadata of the video which is also called search engine optimization. It depends on the title, keywords, description, and tags. I used the vidIQ a chrome extension for SEO. It shows the score for my videos. Please maintain your score above 46.

2) Use compelling titles for videos. Create your titles with some of these words such as how to, how I, secrets of. Sometimes use warning titles such as don't sleep before hearing it.Sometimes use an outcome-driven title such as most inspirational composition

3) Hook them with trailer. A new visitor to your channel didn't know about you and your

channel. The only way to hook them is the trailer. Create a trailer for the channel upload it on your homepage.

4) Try to answer the question of your fans. Suppose someone asked you to post your income. Show your income from youtube as video. Fans are more important than content. Try to make one conversation session with your fans.

5) Reply to each and every subscriber comment at least with some emoji. So that they will have gain some energy and motivation. At least they can use it for their WhatsApp status.

6) You need to create a custom subscription link to your channel and paste it in the description and pin it in the comment box. To create a custom

subscription link **your-channel-link here? sub_confirmation=1**

7) Create your thumbnail as a more attractive one. After the title, you will look into the thumbnails only.

8) you need to set a branding watermark in your videos. To create a branding watermark, go to setting in your channel-> channel-> branding.

Print on Demand

Print on demand is a business model that allows you to sell your designs on merch (such as t-shirts, sweatshirts, hats, mugs, etc) directly to customers. Once a customer makes a purchase, the order is sent to a fulfillment company that prints and ships the order directly to the customer.

There are many websites in this field. I personally worked with Teespring, amazon and the red bubble. The approval process in amazon is quite tough. If you get approved, you no need to worry about marketing. But in the case of Teespring and redbubble You should initialize your sales. Once the sales are initialized, they will promote your products.

You need to have designing skills and creativity for this. If you don't have it. Don't worry about it. You can hire a designer from Fiverr and freelancer.com websites. But you need to research the market to find the perfect niches.

Selecting a niche:

Selecting a niche is the most important part of the process. A good niche can produce even $100 a day. Try to select the trending niches according to the season. Find the holiday and festival of the month and upload the design. Also select an evergreen niche such as graduation, birthday, dog lover, etc. but you have to mention your niche particularly. Suppose you have decided to design a dog lover design, you have to produce a design for a particular breed of dog such as pitbull lover, german shepherd lover. So that the buyer can easily find your products.

Promote your products:

Suppose you followed the previous step means, you have a youtube channel. You can use it to promote the products. You didn't have a youtube channel, don't worry about it. Create an Instagram page and post your products on the page with a link to the store on the website. You can easily increase your follower. You can buy the follower. There are many websites for followers. You can even buy 50k followers at 10 to 15 dollars. It is up to you. You can announce a free giveaway in you're your channel or page, it may increase your followers.

To sign up to merch by amazon you need to have a business mail id, USA bank account number, and routing number which you can get in PayPal and Payoneer and Tax Id(PAN card).

To sign up with Teespring and redbubble You need to have paypal account to withdraw your income.

Amazon kdp:

Amazon kdp is the platform to publish the book in paperback and ebook format. You can go with any this format.

You don't need a separate account like merch by amazon. You can simply use your amazon account. You need the tax id. You can directly withdraw the income to your bank account.

Paperback:

You need to be an author to create a book. You can create fun journals, birthday journals, family journals, ruled notebook, etc. There are also called a notebook. Amazon also sells it for you. If you go with the paperback format, maintain at least 100 books in your bookshelf. You can make your interior using bookbeam.io. which is a paid tool. You can pay it on monthly bases or yearly bases. It provides you all the facilities you need to know such as a niche research tool, keyword research tool, and description generator. If you decide to go with this format, use this tool. So that you can create as many books you need.

Tips and tricks

1. Create your cover as much as attractive. Customer mostly impressed by cover images only.

2. Describe your products as much as possible in a crispy way. So the new customer will know about your product.

3. Select a competition-free niche. If you select a less competitive category, your book will automatically get a lower rank even bestseller too.

4. In recent days, family and children journals are booming. To create a fun journal for family and friends.

E-book:

If you go with an e-book, you have a free promotional tool that is provided by Amazon itself. Enroll your book in KDP select to reach more readers. As long as a new reader reads your page, you will get royalty.

Tips and tricks

1. Select an evergreen niche such as cooking, meditation, diet, health, etc. be specific in

your topic. For example: if you select a diet, specify you're your diet plan such as keto. Specifying your niche will rank your higher in the specific category.

2. Same as paperback. Design a catchy cover.

3. Select a compelling title as said in the youtube segment.

4. Create an author central page to group your book. Anyone of your book will get reach to many people. At that time, the viewer will visit your author's central page also. So that you can get free promotion for other books too.

5. Enroll your book in KDP to increase your rank.

Selling an online course

You can say "I am not a topper or I am not brilliant ". You no need to be brilliant or topper to teach an online course. You can teach whatever you know. You can teach about home organizing, gardening, mysteries, baby care, etc. You can also teach about the experience that you have got in about 4 techniques. Making money online is the one of most trending topics nowadays. If you do any of the above business, You probably know about the pro & coins, technique, and resources of the business. Nowadays the internet is everywhere so that the eLearning market also gets boomed. You can make about Print on demand, KDP selling, Making youtube channel or drop shipping.

6. Try to pick evergreen topics such as money earning, Camping, programming languages, etc.

7. Try to make your own notes and pdf.

8. provide free coupons first and increase your student count and ask them to give review. The udemy will automatically boost your course.

9. Likewise, Upload your courses in various platform.

10. Pre sale your course.

Some of you have knowledge of programming languages. You can probably teach them. Udemy is the best way to reach many e-learners.

Tips & tricks:

1. Make your content as clear as possible.

2. Make your presentation as crispy as possible.

3. Try to teach with practical demo.

4. Share the notebook and problem statement to work with.

5. The voice of the video shouls be clear and fluent. If you are not able to do. Hire some professional readers and match the voice through editing.

www.ingramcontent.com/pod-product-compliance
Lightning Source LLC
Chambersburg PA
CBHW071122220526
45467CB00004B/2011